THE GIRL WHO BUILT AN OCEAN

An Artist, an Argonaut, and the True Story of the World's First Aquarium

JESS KEATING • MICHELLE MEE NUTTER

ALFRED A. KNOPF
NEW YORK

The soft fabric fell before her in shimmering waves, and Jeanne couldn't wait to dive in. In her father's hands, tangled thread and supple brown leather became shoes. In her mother's hands, bolts of cloth and bobbins of fiber became dresses.

What could Jeanne create with *her* hands? Could she transform a pile of *nothing* into a beautiful . . . *something*?

Jeanne rolled up her sleeves and set to work.

When she was eighteen, Jeanne journeyed to Paris to become a seamstress.

She stitched. She sewed. She snipped her scissors and created wearable works of art.

Her hands were always busy, piecing and puzzling together color and fabric in captivating new ways.

She made dresses for friends, socialites . . . and even embroidered a dress for an Italian princess. It was as beautiful and bold as a sunrise. Women from far and wide wanted to wear Jeanne's creations.

But adventure was calling. With her fabric,
her scissors, and her new husband,
Jeanne moved to Sicily.

The Mediterranean was unlike
anything she had ever seen before.
    It was a playground,
    a nursery,
    a galaxy . . .
    and a work of art.

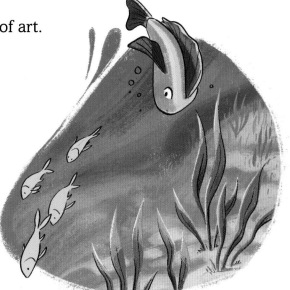

Jeanne wanted to know more
about this enchanting world of
saltwater and sand. So she
rolled up her sleeves once
more and set to work.

She traded her scissors and fabric for seagrass, shells, and the endless shore. Chiffon and taffeta shifted into the foam at her feet as she walked in the sand.

Pearls and sequins
echoed the dappled sunlight
on the horizon.

Jeanne started to collect everything that caught her eye. She kept specimens of minerals and fossils in jars, preserved delicate butterfly wings on paper, and lined her desk with a rainbow of seashells, pebbles, and coral.

Whenever Jeanne found a creature to study,
she observed it carefully each day, taking notes
and sketching its picture in her notebook.
But there was one big problem.

Often, the animals Jeanne wanted to study would quickly say hello, then slip out of view in the deep, dark water.
It is very hard to learn about an animal if you can't see it.

How could Jeanne learn about these mysterious creatures if they kept swimming away?

She considered the puzzle in front of her. She didn't want to study preserved specimens in jars or lose her animals to the shadowy waves.

What she needed was a way to bring the ocean to her. Jeanne rolled up her sleeves to design a solution, using her hands . . .

. . . some glass,

. . . and her imagination.

With these tools, Jeanne built the world's first aquarium.

One aquarium was perfect for her study. Two others were built for the open water, anchored at various depths on the ocean floor.

With her new aquariums, Jeanne was able to observe how elusive animals survived and thrived.

She watched as clams scooted, rolled, and leapt in the current, trickling bubbles to the top of the glass.

She learned that octopuses used stones to pry open tasty mussels.

But one animal fascinated Jeanne more than any other: the argonaut.

Argonauts have eight arms with strong suckers, two eyes, and a sharp beak.
Some of these small octopuses had delicate, translucent shells. But some did not.
Jeanne wondered:

Where did the argonaut get its shell? Many scientists believed that, like hermit crabs, argonauts took their shells from other animals. But no one had caught them in the act. Jeanne wanted to discover the truth.

She rolled up her sleeves once more.

Jeanne collected argonaut eggs from the ocean. Raising them in her aquariums, she took notes, made sketches, and observed them each day.

Some of Jeanne's young argonauts didn't have shells.

Then . . . suddenly they did!

The argonauts weren't finding or stealing shells at all—they were *creating* them! Transforming what appeared to be nothing . . . into a beautiful *something*.

Jeanne even discovered they could repair their shells if they got damaged, using special membranes in their arms.

Jeanne told other scientists about her discovery. Some people didn't believe her. It was unusual for women to study science, but Jeanne never gave up. She shared her argonauts, ten years of careful research, and her incredible aquariums.

The secret behind the argonaut's shell spread
quickly from Italy,
to London,
to the rest of the world.

Through a pane of glass, Jeanne had shed light on one of the ocean's oldest mysteries.

But it was her aquarium—built with her hands, some glass, and her imagination—that brought the ocean to us.

It was her aquarium, beautiful and bold, that changed the world.

BEYOND THE STORY

Jeanne Villepreux (pronounced "veel-PRUH") was a true pioneer in her field. As a woman, she was denied formal training in the sciences, but she didn't let that stop her from exploring the mysteries that sparked her curiosity. She not only asked questions about the world around her, but also devised ways to answer them!

It wasn't easy being a female scientist in her time, and her work was often overlooked because she was a woman. Jeanne persisted, and with the help of a famous naturalist named Richard Owen, she was able to present her incredible research to the scientific community. She is now known as the first person to invent an aquarium that could be used to study live aquatic animals.

Today, Jeanne's groundbreaking work lives on. Whether it's for scientific research, development, food, or conservation, Jeanne's impact—and her aquariums—can be seen worldwide. Scientists even use her innovative method of "restocking" ecosystems, by using aquariums to breed baby fish for release into the wild to help their species survive.

Jeanne's curious nature didn't stop there. She was also the first person to observe octopuses using stones as tools to open fan mussels. It was a remarkable discovery, but her work was cut short when disaster struck. In 1843, a ship carrying her research, collections, and papers was caught in a storm. The ship sank, taking her life's work to the bottom of the ocean. She and her husband were safe, having traveled by land. But it would be many years before her name began to resurface in the public eye.

Could Jeanne have suspected that her creations would live on to this day? We'll never know. But I like to think that, after years watching her precious argonauts build their shells, Jeanne understood the power of invention. By rolling up her sleeves and setting to work, she created something that would change the world forever.

HOW DOES AN ARGONAUT USE ITS SHELL?

Jeanne noted in her research that only female argonauts in her aquariums had shells. She was dismissed at the time, but we know today that this is true! Male argonauts are much smaller than females and they don't make shells. Research shows that female argonauts use their shells to trap air bubbles. These bubbles allow the argonauts to stay vertical in water so they can swim efficiently. It's also believed that the thin shells protect the argonaut's eggs before they hatch.

A TIMELINE OF JEANNE'S LIFE & WORK

1812 – Jeanne journeys to Paris (over 250 miles on foot!) to become a dressmaker and embroiderer.

September 24, 1794 – Jeanne is born in Juillac, France.

1816 – Jeanne creates a wedding dress for Princess Caroline. It is around this time that she meets James Power, a wealthy English merchant.

1818 – Jeanne marries James Power and, soon after, they move to Sicily. It is here that Jeanne begins teaching herself natural history.

1832 to (roughly) **1843** – Jeanne continues to improve on her aquarium designs, creating aquariums that can be submerged in the water at various depths.

1833 – Jeanne discovers through aquarium experiments that argonauts not only build their shells, but can also repair them!

1832 – Jeanne invents the first aquarium.

1843 – Disaster strikes when a ship carrying her life's writings and papers sinks at sea.

1997 – As her work gains wider recognition, a large crater on Venus is named in honor of her achievements.

1834 – Jeanne is elected to the Gioenia Academy of Catania as their first female member.

1858 – Richard Owen (a famous naturalist) names Jeanne "the mother of aquariophily."

1870 – Jeanne flees to her hometown of Juillac during the Franco-Prussian War.

1871 – At the age of 76, Jeanne passes away in Juillac, France.

2022 – Jeanne is honored in the book *The Girl Who Built an Ocean*, which is now in your hands!

1839 – Her first book, *Observations et expériences physiques sur plusieurs animaux marins et terrestres,* is published. (The title translates to "Observations and Physical Experiments on Various Marine and Terrestrial Animals.")